St. Teresa's Own Words:

Or, Instructions on The Prayer of Recollection

Arranged from Chapters 28 and 29 of her *Way of Perfection* for the use of the Sisters of Our Lady of Mount Carmel, Darlington, by

JAMES,

BISHOP OF HEXHAM & NEWCASTLE

Christt
the King
Library

Qui Legit Intelligat
Let he who read understand

St. Teresa's Own Words.

I.

Nature and Definition of the Prayer of Recollection.

IT is called the Prayer of Recollection because in it the soul *collects*, or gathers together, all her powers, and enters into her own interior with God.

I wish I knew how to describe to you this holy intercourse which, without disturbing in the least her perfect solitude, is carried on between the soul and her Divine Spouse and Companion, the Holy of Holies, and which takes place as often as ever she pleases to enter into this interior paradise in company with her God, and to shut the gate to all the world

besides.   I say, as often as she pleases;
for you must understand that this is
not altogether a supernatural thing,
but is quite within our own power,
and we can do it whenever we chose ;
I mean, of course, with God's help,
for without this we can do nothing at
all, not so much as have a single good
thought.   For you must observe that
this recollection is not a suspension of
the powers of the soul, but only a
shutting them up, as it were, within
ourselves.

II.

*The Truth or Foundation on which the
Prayer of Recollection rests:*

You know that God is everywhere
(therefore He is in our interior.) Now
it is clear that wherever the King is,
there the Court is too ; therefore,
wherever God is, there is heaven ;
and you can readily . believe that
wherever this Divine Majesty is, all.
glory is with Him.   Then consider

what St. Augustine says : that he
" sought God in many places, and
found Him at last within himself."

It is, then, of the utmost importance
to bear this truth in mind, that our
Lord is within us, and that we ought
to strive to be there with him.

On a certain occasion, when I was
assisting at the Divine Office with the
rest of the Sisters, I became, on a
sudden, thus recollected within myself and here my own soul was pre-
sented before me, and it seemed to
me to resemble a bright mirror, in
which there was no darkness nor
shadow, either behind or on either
side, or above or below but all clear
and resplendent ; and in the midst of
it there appeared Christ our Lord, in
the form under which I am accustomed
to see Him.   It seemed to me that His
Image was shining forth from every
part of my soul, as though reflected
in the mirror ; and then, by a wonderful communication of love, which I
know not how to describe, this same
mirror of my soul seemed to be re-
produced and again represented, in a

wondrous manner, within the Form of my Divine Redeemer.

[Again], on a certain occasion, it was shown to me that my soul was like a sponge in the midst of the ocean of the Divinity, and that it drank in this heavenly substance, so as, in a manner, to embrace within it the Three Divine Persons.   But, at the same time, I was admonished that though I had the Divinity within my soul, yet I myself was much more contained in Him than He in me.   Thus, whilst I beheld, as it were, hidden within me the Three Divine Persons, I saw that They, at the same time, communicated Themselves to all created things, without ceasing for an instant to abide in me.

On another occasion I was made to understand this truth with great clearness—that all things are seen in God, and that He contains everything within Himself.   I do not know how to describe this ; but it has remained deeply impressed upon my mind, and is one of the greatest favours our Lord has ever granted me, and one that has filled me, more than any other, with confusion at the remembrance of my sins. If it had pleased our Lord to let me see this before I had sinned, or if others, who offend Him, could only have seen it, I believe that neither they nor I would have ever had the boldness to commit sin. No words that I can use can convey any idea of this sublime truth. The only notion I can give of it is this : I beheld the Divinity like a most brilliant diamond, far greater than the whole world, and containing everything within itself ; and in this diamond was reflected, as it were, everything that is done here below. Wonderful it was, indeed, to behold in so short a time, within this glorious mirror, such a multitude of things assembled together ! But to see represented in this pure and unsullied brightness such foul abominations as my sins was a spectacle that fills me with the deepest sorrow whenever I call it to mind. In truth, when I reflect upon it, I know not how I can bear the thought; and at the time when I beheld it, I was so covered with confusion that I did not know which way to turn.

Now it seems to me that this vision may be of much profit to those who are practising this Prayer of Recollection, to teach them to consider our Lord in the interior of their own souls ; for, to repeat what I have so often said before, this consideration fixes the attention far better, and is far more profitable, than to represent Him in any other way.   If, instead of this, we direct our thoughts to God in heaven, or if, in fine, we turn to any spot beyond ourselves, we do but weary our minds and distract our souls, and, after all, lose much of the fruit of our labour.

[In another place,* the Saint says] The soul of the just man is nothing less than a paradise, in which God finds His delight.   And what sort of an abode must that be in which a King so powerful, so wise, so bright and stainless, so rich in every good, delights to dwell !

I can find nothing to which I can compare the great beauty and immense

* *Castle of the Soul*, chap. i.

capacity of a soul.   And, indeed, since God has made our souls, as He tells us, to His own image and likeness, it is not to be expected that our minds, however gifted, should be able to understand the beauty of a soul, any more than we can understand God himself.   To try to do so would be labour in vain; for though there be an immense difference between the Soul and God —the soul being a creature and God her Creator—still, since His Divine Majesty has made the soul to His own image, how great must be its dignity, how surpassing its beauty !

It is a sad pity, and a shame as well, that we do not know ourselves and what we are.   Would it not be thought strange ignorance if, when a man were asked his name or the name of his father or mother, or the land of his birth, he should know nothing about it? But it is a stupidity greater than this beyond comparison to be ignorant of what we are ourselves—to know nothing about it, beyond a general notion that we are living in a body, and that we have a soul; and to think but little of the goods this soul may possess, or Him who dwells within it, and of its exceeding value ; and, hence, to take such little pains to preserve its beauty.

O, that I could teach this truth to those who commit so many foul and shameful sins, that so they might remember that they are not hidden nor out of sight when they do such things ! For, since we are in the immediate presence of His Divine Majesty, He clearly beholds whatever we do ; and yet we presume to behave with such insulting irreverence before His eyes ! I saw how richly hell is deserved for any one single mortal sin ; for it is an evil, great beyond all comprehension, to commit such things in the very Presence of such a Majesty, and it is impossible for any one to understand how opposed they are to His adorable purity.

I was given to understand that, when a soul is in mortal sin, this mirror [see page 6] is, as it were, covered with a thick cloud, and becomes so black that the image of our Lord can neither be represented nor seen in it, although He is still present within the soul, giving her life and being. And when a soul is in heresy, it is as though the mirror were shattered to pieces, which is far worse than being darkened and obscured. But there is a great difference between seeing all this and expressing it in words; for it is very difficult to describe. However, it has been of great advantage to me, and has made me think with a deep sorrow upon the time when, by my sins, I so obscured my soul that I could see my Divine Master there no more.

In how clear a light does it display His infinite mercy, that He should bear with us although, knowing this truth, we still offend Him! And if the mere sight of what I have described filled my soul with such consternation, I cannot but reflect how terrible the Day of Judgment will be when this Sovereign Majesty will reveal Himself to our eyes, and we shall see clearly the sins whereby we have offended Him.

Good God! into what blindness had

I fallen when I sinned against Thee! Many a time have I trembled with terror while writing these lines. And no wonder! The wonder rather is that I should not die at once when I call to mind the things that I have seen, and look upon the life I have led. Blessed be He for evermore who has borne with me so long!

III.

Method and Practice of the Prayer of Recollection.

And now we must see how we can enter into this beautiful and delightful dwelling. It may, perhaps, seem foolish to talk of entering into it ; for, if this dwelling be our own souls, we cannot enter into what is, in fact, ourselves, just as it would be folly to tell a person to enter a room when he was inside it already. But we must understand that there are more ways than one of being inside our souls. There are many, indeed, who do no more than, like a troop of guards, walk round this castle of their souls, and never care to enter it at all, and know nothing about what it contains. Now the gate whereby we have to enter this precious dwelling of our souls is by prayer and consideration. I do not say mental prayer only, but vocal as well, provided it be accompanied with consideration or attention of the mind ; since, without this, it would not be prayer. For if a person does not think who it is that he is speaking to, or what he is asking, or who he is that is praying, or to whom he prays, I certainly do not call that a prayer, how much soever the man may move his lips.*

1. Well, then, you must begin by fixing this truth in your minds : that there is within you a palace of surpassing splendour, whose whole structure is composed of gold and most precious stones—such, indeed, as is fitting for the great King who resides within it ; and that the beauty of your own soul is, in part, the cause why

* *Castle of the Soul*, chap. i.

this palace is so beautiful. For it is most true that no building can be compared, in beauty and magnificence, with a soul that is pure and filled with virtues; and the higher these virtues are, the larger and more resplendent are the jewels that adorn her interior dwelling. And in the midst of this palace dwells the great King who deigns to be your constant guest, and here He sits upon a throne of priceless value, and this throne is in your own heart.

2. But here comes the great point of all. We, on our part, must, with a full and hearty determination, make over to Him entirely this interior palace, that so He may find no difficulty in dealing with it just as with His own property, turning out and putting in whatever He pleases. He has made this an essential condition to the bargain, and certainly His Divine Majesty is quite in the right to do so. Let us not, then, refuse Him what He asks. At the same time He does not force our wills, but He will deign to receive as much as we choose

to give Him ; only remember, *He will never give Himself entirely to us until we have given ourselves entirely to Him.* This is as certain as anything can be, and so important too, that it is for this reason I so often put you in mind of it. Without this He never works those effects in the soul which He does when she is entirely His, without any reserve or obstacle. Nor, indeed, do I well see how He can, for He is a special friend to order and propriety. So that if we fill this palace with all sorts of rabble, and instead of ornament, disfigure it with trifles and worthless trinkets, how is it possible that our Lord can dwell there with all His Court? I am sure it is as much as we can expect if He stays there ever so short a time, in the midst of such confusion.

3. I beseech you, for the love of God, to make no account of earthly favours. Let each one try to do her duty, and if her Superior gives no sign of approbation of her conduct, let her rest assured that our Lord will approve and repay her well. Did we

come into the world to seek our reward in this life? Let our thoughts be ever fixed upon the things that last, and let us make no account of the things here below, for they do not last even for the short space of our lives.

Give no place to thoughts of what others may think of you, for though they may seem but a slight matter at first, yet by degrees they will come to give you much disquiet. Banish them, therefore, at once, remembering that your kingdom is not of this world, and that all visible things will very soon have an end. Endeavour to rise above this, and be content that men should continue to think as they do; remain humble and despised, and be glad to remain so, for the love of your Lord who dwells within you.

Cast your eyes upon yourselves, and not upon others, and look into your own interior in the manner I have described, and there you will find your Heavenly Master, who will never desert you. And the less external consolation you find, the greater will be the tenderness with which He will treat you. He is most tender and compassionate, and never abandons those who are afflicted and despised, if they will but trust in Him alone. Hence the Royal Prophet says "that the Lord is with those who are in affliction." Do you believe this, or not? If you do so, why do you torment yourselves?

O, God of my heart, if we only knew Thee truly and indeed, nothing in the world could distress or trouble us, for Thou art liberal beyond expression to those who wish to put their trust in Thee. Believe me, it is a great point to understand this truth, and to see that all favours and honours here below are nothing but deceit when they turn away the soul from this interior recollection. Good God! who shall be able to teach you to understand this truth as you ought? Certainly not I; for though no one is more bound to understand it than I am, still I have not yet learnt it as it ought to be learnt.

4. We should try to disengage our-

selves, as far as may be, from exterior occupations, that we may occupy ourselves more easily with God in our own interior.

5. And even when engaged with these occupations, we should often turn our thoughts within ourselves, if it be only for a single moment. The mere act of calling to mind what a Companion we have within us, is of great importance.

6. We must try to use our external senses so as to promote the interests of our interior. For example, if we speak to any one, let us call to mind that there is One with whom we may converse in the interior of our souls. If we hear others speak of us, let us remember that there is One to whom we may listen, who speaks to us far more clearly and intimately. Shut yourselves up within this little heaven of your souls, where He ever dwells who made both the heaven within them and the earth without, and accustom yourselves to take off your eyes, and to withdraw from those things by which your external senses are distracted.

7. But, above all things, I want to impress upon you that, when we are speaking to Him we should look at Him and remain in His presence, and not turn our backs upon him; for it seems to me that this is just what we do if, while we are speaking to Him, we are thinking of a thousand absurdities. The whole mischief lies here, that we do not fully understand how near He is to us, but represent Him as far away. And far enough off indeed He would be if we had to go to heaven to see Him. O God, is there, then, so little beauty in Thy countenance that it is not worth looking at when Thou art so near us? When we speak to men we think they are not listening to us if we do not see that their eyes are upon us; and shall we be so blind as not to see that Thou art looking upon us when we are speaking to Thee? How, then, can we know whether Thou hast heard what we have said to Thee? It is, then, of no small importance for a distracted soul to understand this truth, and to see that, in order to speak to her Eternal

Father, and to enjoy His company, there is no need of going up to heaven, or of raising her voice, as though He were afar off. No; however low we speak, so near He is that He is sure to hear us ; nor is there any need of wings to fly and seek Him. Nothing more is required than to place ourselves in solitude, to look at Him within ourselves, and be careful not to turn our eyes away from so amiable a Guest—to collect all our external senses together, to turn them within ourselves, and to give them something to occupy them there.

Let us be convinced that, if we please, we need never be separated from His sweet company. And let us think over with sorrow how, time after time, we have left our Father in His dwelling alone and forgotten — this Father on whose tender support we entirely depend. Let us do this, if we can, many times in the day ; if not so often, at least now and then ; but whether seldom or often, if we do but try we shall find the fruit of it sooner or later.

Speak to Him as to a father, ask Him favours as from a father ; let us tell Him all our troubles, and beg of Him to relieve us, all the while bearing in mind that we are not worthy to be His children. Treat with Him as with your father, your brother, your Lord, and your spouse—sometimes in one way, sometimes in another, for He will teach you what you must do to please Him. Do not act foolishly (with levity) towards Him ; but ask Him with confidence to keep the promises He has made you, and, as He is your Spouse, beg Him to treat you as such. He will soon become so familiar with us as to understand us, as they say, by signs ; so that if we have to say a number of " Our Fathers," He will let us know that He has heard us by the time we have got through a single one. He is always very glad to lessen our labours ; so that if, during a whole hour, we were to say but one " Our Father," yet, provided we (a) bear in mind that we are with Him, and (b) remember that we are asking for Him, and (c) how glad He is to give us what we ask, and (d) how delighted He is to be in our company, He is quite satisfied, and does not wish us to split our heads by trying to make long discourses.

8. The soul thus recollected within herself can also think of the Passion, and represent the Son of God as present within her, and offer Him there to His Father, without wearying her understanding by going and seeking Him on Mount Calvary, or in the Garden, or fastened to the pillar.

9. We can use the method of Prayer of Recollection in praying also to the Saints; for do you suppose that when He comes, He comes by Himself? No; I can be bold to say that His courtiers never leave Him alone, but are with Him wherever He resides, and moreover, are ever making intercession with Him for us, for they are full of charity.

10. Whoever wishes to acquire this habit—for, as I said before, it is entirely within our power—let him not fail to exercise himself daily in

the way I have described. It will give him, little by little, a perfect command over himself. He must give himself wholly to God, it is true ; but this sacrifice is not made for nothing, for in return he receives an entire control over himself and all his faculties. Labour, as nothing worth having is got without it. Persevere in spite of trouble.

11. At the same time we must never lose sight of this truth that the whole of our perfection must be based on humility, and if this humility be not true and sincere, our Lord will never permit the edifice to rise very high. And this in reality is all the better for us, for it would only rise to fall again to the ground ; and the higher it had risen the greater would be the fall. In order, therefore, to build on this solid foundation, let each one try to look upon herself as below her companions rather than above them in point of virtue and excellence. Moreover, let each one be ever on the watch for opportunities to do any little service she can to those around

her, bearing in mind that, in thus serving others, she is doing herself a far greater service than she is rendering to them. For she is thus laying down stones for the foundation of a building, that no danger or temptation will be able to shake.

IV.

Advantages of Using the Prayer of Recollection.

1. It is a great help to a distracted soul (as said before) ; for in order to speak to her Eternal Father and to enjoy His company, there is no need of going up to heaven or of raising her voice, as though He were afar off.

2. This method of prayer, though it be vocal, enables the mind to keep recollected far more easily than in any other way, and brings along with it many excellent fruits.

3. Her (the soul's) Divine Master forms and teaches her far more quickly by this method than if she followed any other way.

4. And leads her much sooner to the prayer of quiet.

5. Those who practise it may rest assured that they are following an excellent way, and that at last they will be allowed to drink at the fount of perfect contemplation.

6. For they will advance much in a very short time. It is like sailing in a ship to one's journey's end. If the wind and weather be favourable, he who travels by water reaches the end of his voyage in a very few days, while he who goes by land is a long time on the way. In the same manner, those who use the Prayer of Recollection are embarked, so to speak, on the sea, and though they have not yet altogether quitted the shore, yet by this recollection of their senses they are doing their best to leave it behind them.

7. Admirable indeed it is, for they who travel by this path are very secure from the dangers which surround them.

8. And the fire of Divine love is easily enkindled within them ; for they

are so very near this heavenly fire that, if their understanding do but breathe upon it, the least spark that touches them inflames their whole souls at once. For since they are not embarrassed by any external thing, but the soul is here alone with her God, they are fully prepared to receive the communication of this Divine fire.

9. In this manner we shall be able to pray vocally with great peace and recollection, and thus be freed from a vast amount of trouble we should otherwise have.

10. For my part, I (St. Teresa) acknowledge that I never knew what it was to pray with satisfaction till our Lord taught me this method ; and the great profit I have always found from this habit of recollecting myself in my own interior has induced me to speak of it so much at length.

11. When our Lord shall have given us this habit of prayer, we shall see so clearly its inestimable value that we shall not be willing to exchange it for all the treasures of the world.

12. I know for certain that, if you will only persevere, in the course of a year, or perhaps in six months, by God's help, you will obtain what you desire. See how short a time is required for obtaining so immense a good!

13. It is no less than laying a solid foundation, upon which the highest perfection of virtue may be built.

I beseech you, therefore, to consider as well spent whatever labour or trouble you may employ upon this great object.

V

Notanda Regarding the Prayer of Recollection.

Let me warn you not to imagine that prayer alone, whether vocal or mental, will serve as a foundation for your spiritual edifice. For unless with this you obtain solid virtues and practise them, you will never advance towards perfection. And would to

God your not advancing were the only evil! But you surely know that he that does not advance is sure to go back, for I do not conceive it possible that love should continue in the same degree without either increasing or growing cold. Unite, therefore, the practice of solid virtue with this interior recollection, so that, if God wishes to raise you to great things, He will find you well prepared, being already so closely united to Himself.

And here let me caution you against a certain false modesty which some people have, and think it humility. Truly it is no humility to refuse a favour which a king offers us! On the contrary, true humility would receive it with an acknowledgment that it is more than we deserve, and be very glad to have got it. A fine sort of humility, when the Lord of heaven and earth has come into my house, with the intention of offering me favours and of taking pleasure in my company, to refuse to answer Him a word, or to stay with Him at all, or to receive what He offers me, and leave Him quite by Himself! Nay, and when He tells me, and even implores me, to ask Him favours, to choose, through humility, forsooth, to remain poor, and even to let Him go away altogether, because He sees that I cannot make up my mind to say anything to Him! Pray, have nothing to do with such humility as this.

Perhaps some persons may think it foolish to explain this matter by such a comparison [as that of the interior mansion.] But I assure you it may help you very much. And more particularly for those who are unlearned, all this is quite necessary to make them understand that there is something within them incomparably more precious than they can see without. Let us not then imagine that we are empty in our own interior. But would to God that there were none but the ignorant who forget this great truth; for if all of us were careful to bear in mind what a Guest we have residing within us, I hold it to be impossible that we should give ourselves up as much as we do to the things of the world, since we should clearly see how contemptible they are when compared with what we possess within ourselves. For if we are ever running after things that gratify our external senses, what else do brute beasts do? When they see an object that pleases their eyes, they seize and devour it to satisfy their hunger. Is there, then, to be no difference between them and us?

Now perhaps there are some people who will laugh at me for being so particular in insisting upon all this, and say, "It is all clear enough." Well, they are quite right; so it is; but yet there was a time when it was very obscure to me. I knew very well that I had got a soul; but as to the value of this soul, and who it was that dwelt within it, about this I knew nothing at all. I had so blinded my eyes with the vanities of the world that I could not see these truths. It seems to me that if I had understood then, as I do now, that so great a King resided in this palace of my soul, I should not have left Him alone so very often, but should have sometimes kept Him company, and should have tried more to purify my soul. For what could possibly excite in a soul such wonder and admiration as this—that He whose greatness would fill a thousand worlds should shut Himself up in so small and mean a dwelling? It was even thus that He was pleased to take up His abode in the womb of His most holy Mother! But as He is the Lord of all, He is free to do whatever He will; and so, because He loves us, He accommodates Himself to our littleness. Thus, when a soul is but beginning, in order that she may not be disturbed by seeing how very little she is to contain One who is so great, He does not allow her, at first, to understand all this, till, little by little, He has enlarged and expanded the soul, according to the measure of those gifts which He designs to bestow upon her. For this reason, I said that He is free to do whatsoever He will, for He has the power to enlarge this palace in which He is pleased to dwell.

Now, if this recollection be real and genuine, it soon shows itself very clearly, for then a certain effect is produced in the soul, which I do not know exactly how to describe, but which is easily understood by one who has felt it. The soul sees that all the things of this world are a mere game, an idle pastime, and joyfully abandons the distracting scene, and then, like one who retires into a strong castle to be out of the reach of his enemies, she withdraws her senses from these external things, and so completely turns her back upon them that, without thinking of it, the eyes of the body close of themselves, that she may see them no longer, but may be better able to attend to what is going on in her own interior. Hence it is that whosoever practises this method almost always has his eyes shut when he is saying his prayers; and this is an excellent custom for many reasons, since it implies the doing some violence to oneself thus to turn away our eyes from these earthly things. However, this effort is only required in the beginning; afterwards there is no need of it, for after a little practice it would be necessary to do oneself a great deal more violence to open the eyes during prayer than to keep them shut. Thus the soul gathers strength and force at the expense of the body. She leaves it, as it were, alone and helpless, and thereby acquires fresh power to govern it and oppose its desires.

Now you must understand that there are various degrees in this recollection; so although, at the beginning, all that I have described may not be clearly felt, yet let us only persevere, in spite of the trouble it may cost us at first, and we shall soon see the advantage of it. I say it will cost us some trouble at first, because the body will try for a time to insist on its rights, not knowing that, by refusing to yield at once, it is its own greater enemy; but if we only persevere for a few days, and do ourselves a little violence, we shall soon perceive the fruit of our exertions. We shall find, as soon as we begin to pray, that the bees will all flock into the hive and set to work to make the honey, and this without any trouble on our part. For it has pleased our Lord to ordain that, in reward for the little trouble we take at the beginning, our understanding and our will receive so complete a mastery over all our powers that if they merely give a sign that they wish to be recollected, the senses obey them at once, and become recollected along with them.

And although, after this, they may again try to run away, yet it is a great point gained to have made them surrender at first; for then they can only steal off like so many captives and conquered subjects, and cannot do us the harm they would have done before; and when the will turns round and calls them all in again, they come back much more quickly. And, at last, after they have thus many times deserted and been brought back again to their post, it pleases our Lord to appoint that they remain at rest for good and all in perfect contemplation.

I would have you clearly to understand what I have said. Although it may seem obscure at first, every one will soon comprehend it if he will only try to practise it. I pray His Divine Majesty never to permit us to withdraw ourselves from His holy presence.

Amen.

PARTICULAR EXAMEN

*As to how we Use the Prayer of Recollection.**

1. Do I, when commencing, make an act of lively Faith in the presence of God in my interior?

2. Do I humble myself before Him and ask His help?

3. Do I make efforts to collect the powers of my soul, to take off my exterior senses, and to turn both one and the other on our Lord in my interior, by looking at and listening to

* By Bishop Chadwick.

Him, and by believing that He is both looking at and listening to me, and that He is close at hand?

4. Have I seated Him on His throne in my interior, *i.e.*, on my heart, viz., my will and affections?

5. Have I often declared to Him that I desire to give myself entirely to Him, *and do I so give myself?*

6. Do I treat Him familiarly, but without levity, styling Him Father, Brother, Spouse, &c., making known to Him my wants, declaring that I am His spouse, and that He is to treat me as such, bearing in mind that I am with Him, and He with me, that He is glad to give me what I ask, and that He delights to be with me?

7. Do I ask Him for what I stand in need of, and speak to Him with faith, desire, confidence, humility, perseverance, declaring on my part that I will do all He requires in order that I may obtain what I ask?

8. Do I make practical resolutions? What are they, and do I beg His blessing on them?

9. Do I practise Prayer of Recollection daily?

10. Do I give way to distractions? If so, what are the sources of them? Am I resolved to cut these sources off?

11. Do I thank our Lord before rising from prayer, and take care not to dissipate my interior by wilful negligence?

12. Is my prayer *fruitful?*—*i.e.* (*a*) Do I increase in a desire to advance in solid virtue and in perfection? (*b*) Do I endeavour, in great peace, to lessen the number of my faults and imperfections? (*c*) Do I endeavour to practise the solid virtues? (*d*) Is my desire for sincere humility on the increase?

13. Do I, from time to time, read and ponder over St. Teresa's instructions on the Prayer of Recollection?

Made in the USA
Coppell, TX
05 January 2022

70931321R00024